SPIRITUAL THORNS

FROM

THE SEEDS OF DIVORCE

By
Jimmy H. Hampton

TABLE OF CONTENTS

INTRODUCTION

CHAPTERS

INTRODUCTION

This book is written to Christian couples who are having marital issues, who may be contemplating divorce, who may already be separated, and couples who have divorced but not remarried.

God's institution of marriage, man and woman becoming one flesh, is taught from the Word. God's love for families is reflected upon. The institution of marriage is scripturally described.

God hates divorce per the Scriptures. The reality of the consequences of divorce is taught. Divorce breeds divorce. Divorce creates permanent storm clouds of life in the lives of the couple, in the lives of their children, and in the lives of their grandchildren that are still in the loins of their children. Divorce begins a cycle of divorce and remarriage that never ends until a descendant of the couple determines to break the cycle and remains married for life.

Couples are encouraged to place the best interest of their children over their personal interest. The here-and-now damages of life, the life-time damages that seem to never end, and the eternal damage that divorce reeks upon the children are revealed.

Men are taught how divorce terminates their scriptural ability to serve as an elder or deacon in the Lord's church.

The harvest of divorce is taught in all of its ugliness and reality. The spiritual thorns from the seeds of divorce are disclosed.

This book is written in love for you parent's souls and the souls of your children. The book was not written to make you "feel good" but to share with you the reality of divorce and hopefully encourage you to disregard divorce as an option for your marital issues.

The book closes with encouragement for couples to forgive, reconcile, and restore. Couples are encouraged to keep their families together and to claim a victory over the demon called divorce.

CHAPTER 1

GOD INSTITUTED MARRIAGE

God created woman (Eve) and brought her to man (Adam). Man called her Woman because she was taken out of Man (Genesis 2:21-23). And then the Scripture speaks, **"For this reason a man shall leave his father and his mother, and be joined to his wife; and they shall become one flesh"** (Genesis 2:24). God created man and woman to be bound together in holy union, therefore, God instituted and ordained marriage between man and woman.

Marriage is a covenant between a man and a woman, a covenant recognized by the creator of marriage, God Himself. Malachi speaks of the covenant between husband and wife.₁ Jesus taught that husband and wife should become one flesh. Listen to Jesus speak:

> **"...Have you not read that He who created** *them* **From the beginning MADE THEM MALE AND FEMALE,**
> **And said, 'FOR THIS REASON A MAN SHALL LEAVE HIS FATHER AND MOTHER AND BE JOINED TO HIS WIFE, AND THE TWO SHALL BECOME ONE FLESH'?**
> **So they are no longer two, but one flesh. What therefore God has joined together, let no man separate"**
> (Matthew 19:4-6).

Why marry? The apostle Paul answered this question. Paul said in order for man and woman to avoid the sin of fornication that each man is to have his own wife and each woman is to have their own husband.[2]   God created man and woman with hormones and a sex drive. God intends for men and women to enjoy that physical blessing by them participating in sexual activity according to His design and His will that is found in His Word.

God's design for mankind's sexual activity is for the relationship to be between male and female in marriage. The Lord spoke His statutes and ordinances to Moses and He instructed Moses to teach them to the children of Israel.   There were many ordinances governing men and women's sexual relationships (Leviticus 18-20). The Lord said that if a man lies with a male as those who lie with a woman, they both commit a detestable act and would be put to death.[3]   The Scriptures state that no homosexuals will be in Heaven.[4]

God's will for how men and women are to conduct their sex lives is quite simple and easy to understand. Any sexual intercourse other than between husband and wife is fornication.   Fornication is sin. There will be no fornicators in Heaven.[4] When a husband or a wife has sexual intercourse outside of marriage, they commit adultery. Adultery is sin and the punishment for adultery is eternal death in Hell.[4]

God gave man the ability to enjoy his wife's body and He gave woman the ability to enjoy her husband's body through intercourse. Paul taught that,

"The husband must fulfill his duty to his wife, and likewise also the wife to her husband" (I Corinthians 7:3). Paul said that the husband and wife should not deprive themselves of one another except by agreement for a time to devote themselves to prayer and then come back together so that satan will not tempt them because of lack of self-control.5

God created man with the ability to reproduce man, thereby multiplying and replenishing mankind upon earth.6 Man's reproduction of man is to be within the institution of marriage. God takes the sperm of the man and the egg of the woman and creates a beautiful, precious baby boy or girl. God created man and woman to marry and to have a family and for their offspring to reproduce. He loves families.

THE MARRIAGE RELATIONSHIP

The marriage relationship between man and woman is so precious in the eyes of the Lord that He instructed for THE MARRIAGE TO MIRROR CHRIST'S CHURCH. The apostle Paul who was inspired by the Holy Spirit compared marriage to Christ and the church. I encourage you to study the 5th chapter of Ephesians with your spouse to learn how your marriage is to compare with the church. We will now highlight Paul's teachings.

➢ Wives are to be subject to their husbands as to the Lord.

➢ The husband is the head of the wife as Christ is the head of the church. Paul wrote to the Corinthians that Christ is the head of every man, and the man is the head of a woman, and God is the head of Christ (1 Corinthians 11:3).

➢ As the church is subject to Christ, so also wives ought to be subject to their husbands in everything.

➢ Husbands, you are to love your wives, just as Christ also loved the church and gave himself for her [the church].

➢ Husbands are to love their wives as their own bodies.

➢ He who loves his own wife, loves himself.

➢ No one ever hated his own flesh, but nourishes and cherishes it, just as Christ also does the church.

The marriage union that is in harmony with God's will is holy in the sight of God and our Lord Jesus Christ. Marriage is the only institution on earth that is to be a mirror reflection of the church. God places such great spiritual value upon marriage that marriage becomes a divine institution of the flesh sanctioned by our Father God.

A MARRIAGE GROUNDED UPON A FOUNDATION OF LOVE will be like a house built on a rock, <u>it will not wash away</u> when the storm clouds of life release a torrential down-pour of trials and tribulations. Paul wrote a short treatise on love in the 13th chapter of 1 Corinthians.

The next few paragraphs come from my book titled "Born Anew! What Now For You?." Sweet brethren, open your bibles now to 1 Corinthians, 13th chapter, and read the entire chapter. The chapter has only 13 verses. Do yourself a great big favor, read this chapter often and refresh your memory about the nature of love and about the absolute necessity of you being consumed in love for God and your fellow man. Those of you who have a gift of memorization, commit this chapter to memory so that this divine teaching on love will be constantly in your heart, mind, and soul.

Now that you have read the chapter, let us talk about it. Paul ended chapter 12 with an encouragement for us to desire the greater spiritual gifts and then he made a statement that leads into his 13 verses on love. He said, **"But earnestly desire the greater gifts. And I show you a still more excellent way"** (1 Corinthians 12:31). Then he began to teach on the vanity of not having love in our life.

Many people have a gift to speak fluently and brilliantly. Men have been elected to the highest governmental office in our land primarily because of their ability to speak and to persuade people with their speeches. Paul teaches us that if we have the ability to speak in this manner and even if we are able to speak as angels and we have not love, we are just noise makers like the cymbals in a musical band. Our beautiful speeches are vanity before the Lord if we have not love in our hearts.

Paul really shakes the core of our heart, mind, and soul in his teaching on love. Please listen to him and remember that he wrote these words through the inspiration of the Holy Spirit. **"If I have the gift of prophecy, and know all mysteries and all knowledge; and if I have all faith, so as to remove mountains, but do not have love, I am nothing"** (1 Corinthians 13:2). Do you hear what Paul is saying? Can you imagine having the gift of prophecy and knowing all mysteries? Can you relate to having all knowledge? What if you could quote from memory all of the Word from Genesis 1:1 to Revelation 22:21? What if your faith was so great that you could move mountains like Jesus spoke about in Matthew 17:20?

Precious Brothers and Sisters in Christ, if we each had the gift of prophecy and all knowledge and mountain moving faith, we would be nothing without love in our hearts for our Father God, our Lord and Savior, Jesus Christ, the Holy Spirit, and one another. We are absolutely nothing if our hearts, minds, and souls are not full and overflowing with love - we are just *'walking clay*!'

Paul addressed our intangible and spiritual possessions in verse 2; in verse 3 he focuses on our tangible or physical possessions and the vanity of not loving. **"And if I give all my possessions to feed the poor, and if I surrender my body to be burned, but do not have love, it profits me nothing"** (1 Corinthians 13:3). Feeding the poor is a Godly deed. God wants us feed the poor, to feed the hungry, to give drink to the thirsty, to put clothes on those who are in need of clothing, to assist in sheltering those without shelter, to always bear one another's burdens. If we sell our homes and furnishings, sell our businesses, sell our farms and cattle, sell our investments, sell our vehicles and give all of the cash proceeds to feed the poor and have not love, we have profited nothing before the Lord. Without love, all of our generosity is in vain.

Paul quickly goes from giving all of our worldly possessions to giving the supreme sacrifice, that of giving our body to be burned. We hear of individuals who pour gasoline on themselves and strike a match for some cause or some protest. A tragedy beyond our imagination would occur if our religious freedom was taken away and government troops came into our Church buildings and forced us at gunpoint into the streets and burned us one by one. But the greatest eternal tragedy would be if there was one among the martyrs who did not love his or her fellow man and hated the ones doing the killing. Without love, the giving of their body to be burned was of no profit to the martyr before the Lord.

Paul begins in verse 4 to communicate the attributes or features of Love. Read this list of attributes and determine if these qualities exist in your life. Perform a 'Love Test' upon yourself.

- Love is patient,
- Love is kind,
- Love is not jealous,
- Love does not brag,
- Love is not arrogant,

- Love does not act unbecomingly,
- Love does not seek its own,
- Love is not provoked,
- Love does not take into account a wrong suffered,
- Love does not rejoice in unrighteousness,
- Love rejoices with the truth,
- Love bears all things,
- Love believes all things,
- Love hopes all things,
- Love endures all things.

"Love never fails; but if there are gifts of prophecy, they will be done away; if there are tongues, they will cease; if there is knowledge, it will be done away" (1 Corinthians 13:8). Love, a fruit of the Holy Spirit, is eternally permanent. Love will never end. Love will accompany us into eternity. We will not be ignorant In Heaven, but we will no longer need the knowledge of this physical world. Our spiritual knowledge will become full and our understanding of God's heavenly realm will be complete when we arrive at our home in heaven. (End of quote from my book, BORN ANEW! WHAT NOW FOR YOU?)

> GOD PLACES SUCH GREAT SPIRITUAL VALUE UPON MARRIAGE THAT MARRIAGE BECOMES A DIVINE INSTITUTION OF THE FLESH SANCTIONED BY OUR FATHER GOD.

Apostle Paul placed great emphasis upon love. He said love was greater than faith and hope, **"But now faith, hope, love, abide these three; but the greatest of these is love"** (1 Corinthians 13:13). Faith, hope, and love are at the very core of our relationship with God and His Son, Jesus Christ. However, love excels over faith and hope. Love must flourish and abound within our mind and spiritual heart. Our faith and hope are in vain if we have not love in our hearts for God, Jesus, the Holy Spirit and our fellow man.

Did you notice that Paul did not mention marital sex in his description of love? However, the love that he described is the love that is alive in the foundation of a healthy, happy marriage. And that love will sustain the marriage and the marriage will survive all of the storm clouds of life.

Please allow us to further explore the nature of love.
- Love knows not envy.
- Love is not seasonal.
- Love is not selfish.
- <u>Love considers your spouse and your children first.</u>
- Love is not artificial.
- Love is understanding.
- Love will go as many miles as necessary to help.
- Love can say "No."
- Love can discipline.
- Love is unconditional.
- Love is sacrificial.

- Love cares.
- Love serves.
- Love is humble.
- Love is dependable.
- Love is faithful.
- Love gives.
- Love speaks in deeds.
- Love is manifested in actions.
- Love loves the unlovable.
- Love looks beyond the body and sees the beauty of the inner man and woman.
- Love expresses itself in true friendship.
- Love is more than words.
- Love sustains.
- Love allows the opinions of others.
- Love does not terminate with disagreement.
- Love remains safe and has no fear.
- Love takes us out of our comfort zone into the lives of others to encourage them to consider the destiny of their souls, to share Jesus with them, to tell them of heaven and hell, and to influence them to choose heaven.
- Love in its fullest was displayed on the cross.
- Our love for Christ is expressed in our obedience to His commandments.
- Our love for God is shown in our servitude to Him.
- Our love for the Holy Spirit is shown in our walk and fellowship with Him.
- Our love for the Word of God is shown in our thirst for knowledge of God's will and our daily study of the Scriptures.

➤ Our love for our church family is evidenced by our always being there for our brothers and sisters in Christ, helping and encouraging them in their daily walk with God and Jesus.
➤ Our love for our lost neighbors prompts us to share the story of Jesus with them in love.
➤ Our love for our spouse is unconditional.

A marriage based and centered upon sex is like a house built on shifting sand, it will not survive the strong winds of life. Sex alone will not form the bond needed between husband and wife for their marriage to sustain their differences, their nuisances, their health issues, their financial difficulties and the list goes on. You know the list. A marriage based upon sex will fail.

Folks, God's two greatest institutions are His Son's church and marriage. You are blessed to have the opportunity to be in both of those divine institutions. *Therefore, be imitators of God, as beloved children; and walk in love, just as Christ also loved you and gave Himself up for us, an offering and a sacrifice to God as a fragrant aroma.*[7] Husbands, love your wives. Wives, love your husbands. Love one another as Christ loved you and died a horrible, painful death especially for you.

This book reveals the consequences of divorce and the eternal damage that divorce wrecks upon your family, even family not yet born. Please read the entire book with an open mind and receptive heart. My prayer for you is that you will realize the consequences of divorce and that you and your spouse will forgive, reconcile, restore, forget, keep your family together and refuse to divorce. I pray that your children will not experience their parent's divorcing.

1 Malachi 2:14
2 1 Corinthians 7:2
3 Leviticus 20:13
4 1 Corinthians 6:9-10
5 1 Corinthians 7:5
6 Genesis 1:28
7 Ephesians 5:1-2

CHAPTER 2

GOD HATES DIVORCE

**" "For I hate divorce," says the Lord,
the God of Israel…"**
(Malachi 2:16).

Why? Why does God hate divorce? You will find the answer to that question as you continue to read the pages of this book.

WARNING! The reality of divorce is shared with you from this point forward.
This message is written to you in love for you and your children.
The message in this book will not make you feel good because divorce is ugly, heartbreaking, and destructive to families and to souls.

Divorce is a demon. Why do I say that divorce is a demon? Anything that destroys a God ordained entity is a demon, a tool of satan. Divorce destroys God's institution of marriage and divorce destroys families. Satan is the power behind divorce. Satan loves divorce for it increases his chances of claiming the souls of the Christian family trapped in the jaws of divorce. Satan already has the families who do not live for God, however, divorce further solidifies his chances of keeping those folks in his camp and he is happy with that.

Satan is a great fisher-of-men who has a tackle box full of lures to cast before God's children. His lures come in the form of drugs, alcohol, pornography, gambling, divorce, greed, sex outside of marriage, good-time partying, happy hour, and the "wants" – wanting more and more of this world's things. Satan promises joy, relief, good times, fulfillment, and happiness to his audience of men and women. His promises sound so good, so alluring, so tempting, but they are so false.

Divorce is spiritual cancer that kills souls. Physical cancer can only kill the body that it abides within and it does not spread throughout the family like the flu, a cold or any contagious disease. Spiritual cancer from divorce rages through the family members like a wild fire or a very infectious disease. The early stage of spiritual cancer spreads immediately to all family members whenever mom and dad start their verbal fighting before the children.

The spiritual cancer grows deeper and deeper into the hearts, minds, and souls of the children as mom and dad progress with their fighting and their threats of separation or divorce. When divorce occurs, the cancer becomes almost irreversible and may lead family members to their second death, eternity spent in Hell.

God hates divorce for many reasons. Following is some of the reasons why God hates divorce:
- ➢ Divorce destroys God's institution of marriage.
- ➢ Divorce destroys families.

➤ Divorce hurts children beyond any measure known to man.

➤ Divorce is discouraging and hurtful to the church family.

➤ Divorce sets in motion a chain reaction of divorces in the future of the children of divorced couples and in their grandchildren yet to be born.

➤ Divorce leaves a hollow hole in the hearts of children that never heals.

➤ Divorce many times cheats the children out of productive, vibrant lives by leading them to drugs, alcohol, sex, children born out of wedlock, discouragement from obtaining a higher education.

➤ Divorce turns many children "OFF" to life. Mom and dad's divorce hurts them so deeply in their hearts, minds, and souls that their world is turned upside down. Some children of divorce never regain their proper balance in life.

➤ Divorce increases the population of prisons. Only God knows the number of children of divorce that have been turned "OFF" by divorce and their subsequent bad choices sent them to prison.

➤ Divorce has a high rate of destroyed souls.

➤ Divorce increases the population of Hell.

> ➢ Divorce burns a brand upon the relationship of a child with their parents. The child cannot mention dad to mom, or mention mom to dad. The child's relationship with their parents becomes very awkward and difficult for the child to cope with.

Divorce in a Christian family creates an environment that opens the door for satan to step in and promote his schemes and claim the souls of family members. Therefore, divorce results in God's plan for the salvation of the family to be in vain. Christ's suffering on the cross and the shedding of His blood was in vain for all of the spiritual fallout souls from divorce.

GOD HATES DIVORCE

Anything that destroys a God ordained institution is a tool of satan, a demon. Divorce destroys God's institution of marriage and divorce destroys families. Divorce is a tool of satan.

Please keep reading.

CHAPTER 3

THERE IS LIFE AFTER A SCRIPTURAL JUSTIFIED DIVORCE

God's institution of marriage is very special in His eyes. He did not create the one-flesh union of man and woman for the marriage bed to be defiled. **"Marriage *is to be held* in honor among all, and the *marriage* bed *is to be* undefiled; for fornicators and adulterers God will judge"** (Hebrews 13:4). Husband and wife must constantly honor their marriage union before God, before Jesus Christ, and before one another. There is no exception or justification for fornication outside of the marriage.

God hates divorce but He provided one justification for divorce, however, that one justification for divorce does not change His attitude towards divorce. Jesus spoke about divorce, **"It hath been said, Whosoever shall put away his wife, let him give her a writing of divorcement;**
But I say unto you, That whosoever shall put away his wife, saving for the cause of fornication, causeth her to commit adultery; and whosoever shall marry her that is divorced committeth adultery" (Matthew 5:31-32, KJV). Jesus stated the one justification for divorce when he said *...saving for the cause of fornication.* The word *saving* is translated *except* in the NASB version. Fornication outside of the marriage by one of the marriage partners gives Scriptural justification for divorce to the innocent spouse.

Jesus later in His ministry spoke on the same subject, **"And I say unto you, Whosoever shall put away his wife, except it be for fornication, and shall marry another, committeth adultery; and whoso marrieth her which is put away doth commit adultery"** (Matthew 19:9, KJV).

The spouse who has Scriptural justification for divorce can have a life with God in His Kingdom after divorce – thanks to His wonderful grace. However, that spouse is not exempt from all of the thorns from the seeds of divorce. The seeds and the resulting harvest of a justified divorce are no different than a divorce that is contrary to God's law. The consequences and possible end results for the justified spouse and the children are the same!

Very little long term good comes from divorce. You may get short term relief from an abusive spouse, relief from a spouse who constantly runs up credit card debt, relief from a spouse's abuse of drugs or alcohol, or relief from a contentious wife. Regardless of the short term relief, you can expect a long-term harvest of heartaches as sure as sunshine follows the rain.

The seeds and the resulting harvest of a justified divorce are no different than a divorce that is contrary to God's law. The consequences and possible end results for the justified spouse and the children are the same! The Spiritual thorns still remain.

CHAPTER 4

DIVORCE BREEDS DIVORCE

Divorce creates a breeding ground for divorce. When children of Christian parents get caught up in the divorce of their parents, their perspective of marriage becomes distorted. Too many of these children grow up with the same attitude that the world has towards marriage. They think marriage is just a relationship to live within as long as things go their way. If it doesn't work, divorce and marry someone else.

The children who live through their parent's divorce will go down one of two roads. They will either be determined to have a successful marriage and not break up their family like their parents did or they will go to the divorce court. A well educated young lady and I were discussing the Christian home and I commented that divorce breeds divorce. She immediately took offense and she said, *"No, divorce does not always breed divorce. My parents divorced and I know what it did to me. I am determined to not divorce. I will not divorce. I will not do that to my children."*

That young lady is in the minority. Divorce is not for her. She does not want her children to be victims of divorce like she was. She is determined for her and her husband to work through all of their marital issues with love for their children and love for one another; and to keep their family together. Christian husbands and wives, please imitate this lady and disregard divorce as a solution to your relationship problems – delete divorce from your minds.

Please understand Christian parents, that if you divorce (regardless of the reason or the justification), you will have ZERO influence over your adult child that announces someday that they are getting a divorce. There is not a word that you can say that will influence them to not divorce. You will reap the harvest of divorce. Your prior actions of divorce will speak louder than your words to your child who is planning divorce.

Dear brother and sister in Christ, your divorce will begin a chain reaction of divorce among your offspring that will go forward into the future even after your death. Your divorce will leave a trail of strained relationships, heartaches, children born out of wedlock, failed marriages, maybe even descendants going to prison, and the great possibility of many lost souls. Is your pending divorce worth all of this?

DIVORCE IS THE DEMISE OF THE FAMILY, THE DEMISE OF THE FAMILY IS THE DEMISE OF THE NATION.

CHAPTER 5

LOVE YOUR CHILDREN

MORE THAN YOU LOVE YOURSELF

"Behold, children are a gift of the Lord,
The fruit of the womb is a reward"
(Psalm 127:3).

Parents, please come to a full understanding and realization that your children will be the real victims of your divorce. Your divorce will change and scar your children's lives for all their days upon this earth, and possibly even into eternity if your divorce causes them to walk away from God. Please, I am begging you to love your children more than you love yourself. Consider your children's best interest over yours and do not divorce.

Divorce is a very selfish act. Divorce among Christian parents is evidence of their selfishness. Christian parents would not divorce if they loved their children more than they love themselves. Divorce would not occur if the parents considered the best interest of their children first. Parents would swallow their selfishness, love their children, love one another, reconcile, and keep their family together if they loved their children more than they love themselves.

LOVE YOUR CHILDREN MORE THAN YOURSELF

Folks, let us reflect upon selfishness for a bit. Selfishness is sin and that is the reason why selfishness destroys. We find that God proclaimed selfishness to be sin under the Old Law. God established that a remission of debts would occur at the end of every seven years. Every creditor was to release what he had loaned to his neighbor and was to never collect the debt because the Lord's remission had been proclaimed. God told the people that if the year of remission was near and their poor brother needed help and they gave him nothing, it was sin on their behalf. [1]

God knew there would be people who would not lend to others as the year of remission grew near because of their selfishness. People knew that if they loaned money to someone close in time to the remission of debt, they would not be repaid. Therefore, God warned those who refused to help their brother that their selfishness was sin.

We go forward in time to the early church. The apostle Paul wrote to the church in Philippi regarding selfishness. Please read and meditate upon Philippians 2:1-4. Paul gave the following instructions in those verses:

- ➢ Do nothing from selfishness (verse 3).
- ➢ Regard one another as more important than yourselves (verse 3).
- ➢ Do not merely look out for your own personal interests (verse 4).
- ➢ Look out for the interest for others (verse 4).

LOVE YOUR CHILDREN MORE THAN
YOURSELF

Christian parents, divorce is totally contrary to Paul's teachings in these verses. Divorce is a selfish act. You will not divorce when you regard your children as more important than yourselves and you look out for their best interest. Precious parents, your children are worth more than any good that you think will come out of divorce.

James, the brother of Jesus, wrote that *where jealousy and selfish ambition exist, there is disorder and every evil thing.*₂ Selfishness is the root cause for many, many divorces. Divorce opens the door for satan to step in and he will definitely step in. He will bring disorder to the family and offer an array of temptations that lead to all sorts of sin.

SELFISHNESS HAS NO ROOM IN THE HOUSE OF MARRIAGE!

Christian fathers, God has given you great responsibility to rear your children in the Lord. The apostle Paul instructed, **"Fathers, do not provoke your children to anger, but bring them up in the discipline and instruction of the Lord"** (Ephesians 6:4). You fathers who are anticipating divorce, you may have brought up your children in the discipline and instruction of the Lord. I hope that you have. That is the responsibility that God placed upon all of us fathers.

Fellows, divorce will cast a shadow upon all that you have taught to your children – a shadow so dark that your children will be exasperated. Paul warned us fathers, **"Fathers, do not exasperate your children, so that they will not lose heart"** (Colossians 3:21). Exasperate is a word that most of us do not use in our every day conversations. Let us consult Webster on the word's definition. Webster defines *exasperate* as "to irritate in a high degree; to arouse angry feelings; to provoke beyond endurance; extremely trying; provoking."

Why does the divorce of Christian parents exasperate their children? Because the children's world comes crashing down around them when their parent's divorce. The children experience a trauma in their lives that they never really heal from. The children's exasperation remains with them for life like a chronic disease. The exasperation from their parent's divorce may wane but it will never die in the hearts and minds of the children.

Christian parents, we will end this chapter with words from Jesus Himself. **"The Son of Man will send forth His angels, and they will gather out of His kingdom all stumbling blocks, and those who commit lawlessness,**

And will throw them into the furnace of fire; in that place there will be weeping and gnashing of teeth" (Matthew 13:41-42). Jesus said that He will send His angels to gather all stumbling blocks out of His kingdom, the Church, and throw them into the fires of Hell. Jesus wasn't speaking to the people of the world who serve satan. He was speaking to those in His church.

Parents, I am not judging you. The consequences of divorce among Christian parents in the past are testimony that your divorce may become a stumbling block to your children. Some children of divorce will overcome but many will not. Do you really want to gamble with the souls of your children and with your souls? Whatever it is that you are expecting to gain from your divorce, is it worth even one soul – whether it be your soul or your child's soul?

THE COST OF DIVORCE CANNOT BE MEASURED IN MONEY. THE COST IS MEASURED BY BROKEN FAMILIES, LIFE-LONG HEARTACHES, AND EVEN SOULS LOST IN HELL.

---

1 Deuteronomy 15:1-2, 9
2 James 3:16

Please do not put the book down. I beg you to keep reading.

CHAPTER 6

MEN, DIVORCE WILL PREVENT YOU FROM QUALIFYING TO SERVE AS AN ELDER OR A DEACON IN THE LORD'S CHURCH

Brothers in Christ, divorce will prevent you from ever serving as an elder or a deacon in the Lord's church. The apostle Paul taught the attributes that a Christian man must possess to serve as an elder or a deacon. Divorce shuts the door for you to enter into the ministry of God ordained church family leadership.

Paul detailed the attributes of an elder and a deacon in 1 Timothy 3:1-12 and elders in Titus 1:5-9. Elders and deacons must be the husbands of only one wife. Brother, if you divorce and remarry, you disqualify yourself from serving as an elder or deacon. You may ask, *"What if I divorce and I do not remarry? Am I still qualified to serve?"*

I will answer your question with a question. Will your divorce be a testimony that you failed to manage your household well? Paul said that an overseer or elder, **"...must be one who manages his own household well, keeping his children under control with all dignity,**
But if a man does not know how to manage his own household, how will he take care of the church of God?" (1 Timothy 3:4-5).

31

Paul was talking to all Christian men including divorcees who have not remarried. Every Christian husband and father has the responsibility to manage their household well and to rear their children in the Lord. A well managed household prior to marital issues will be broken by divorce and the walls of that household will be torn down.

Brothers in Christ, please understand that divorce is more than the termination of a legal relationship in the eyes of the world – divorce immediately transports you into spiritually troubled waters of life. Your divorce will grieve the Holy Spirit that dwells within you. **"Do not grieve the Holy Spirit of God, by whom you were sealed for the day of redemption"** (Ephesians 4:30). God blessed you with the gift of the Holy Spirit when you were baptized into Christ (Acts 2:38). The Holy Spirit is grieved by any action that a Christian takes that is contrary to God's will. We have already established that God hates divorce, therefore, divorce grieves the Holy Spirit.

You can depend upon satan to take advantage of your divorce. He knows that divorce places you upon the sea of spiritually troubled waters of life. He will maneuver in your life and create waves of discouragement to wash you upon the shores of spiritual despair whereby you may become a bench warmer, a non-participant in the church family, or you may completely walk away from the Lord and His church. Brother, please do not enter these troubled waters.

Divorce places you upon the sea of spiritually troubled waters of life. Brother, please do not enter these troubled waters. The storm never really goes away. There are just short periods of calm waters and then comes more waves of heartache. The shadow of divorce will always lurk around you because satan will not let divorce and its consequences die – divorce accomplishes too much for him.

CHAPTER 7

THE HARVEST OF DIVORCE

The Spiritual thorns from the seed of divorce will sting your heart and soul forever, for all eternity. The harvest of divorce will follow you for life. Divorce is not a respecter of persons! NO PERSON IS EXEMPT FROM THE CONSEQUENCES OF DIVORCE. Please do not deceive yourself and think that you and your children will be exempt from the harvest of divorce.

There are many unwritten laws of nature that are part of the world that we live in. We have to learn the laws of nature and live within them to survive life on this earth. One of those laws is that *we reap what we sow, we harvest what we plant.* Let us go to the Scriptures and read regarding this concept. **"According to what I have seen, those who plow iniquity and those who sow trouble harvest it"** (Job 4:8).
"He who sows iniquity will reap vanity…" (Proverbs 22:8). **"For they sow the wind and they reap the whirlwind…"** (Hosea 8:7).

"Do not be deceived, God is not mocked; for whatever a man sows, this he will also reap" (Galatians 6:7, underline added for emphasis). Apostle Paul continues in the next verse and teaches that when one sows to his own flesh, they will from the flesh reap corruption, but when one sows to the Spirit, they will from the Spirit reap eternal life. The act of divorce is definitely not sowing to the Spirit.

<u>Divorce Court</u>:   The Divorce Court Judge decides which parent that children under the age of 18 years will reside with. The Judge assigns custody of the children to a parent and visitation rights are given to the other parent. Sometimes the Judge requires that children appear in the court for him/her to question them about their parents and their home life. This becomes a traumatic experience that no child should be subjected to. It leaves a painful brand burned upon their hearts and memory.

Divorced parents have the tendency to allow their children to do whatever they want in order for the parent to be in good favor with the child. The parents compete with one another for the affection from their children. This promotes the deterioration of discipline and spiritual guidance from the parents. The 'stage becomes set' for the children to grow up in the clutches of satan.

Children are innocent victims of divorce. The children witness their moms and dads separate, one parent moving out of the home, divorce occurring; their home never being the same; their world being turned upside down on them. The hurt that the children encounter penetrates the depth of their hearts and souls. There are no words to adequately describe their hurt.

You can depend upon something to come from the hurt that your children will suffer from your divorce. You can depend upon it as sure as sunshine follows the rain.

Your children's hurt will give satan the opportunity to step in at the opportune time and offer his lures of drugs, alcohol, and companionship (sex outside of marriage). Teenagers and young adults from broken homes have a tendency to turn to alcohol and drugs. I know. How do I know? I teach the gospel of Christ every Monday night to young men in the local Texas prison who have been sentenced to prison for their substance abuse. The majority of the fellows are under 30 years of age. Many of the young men come from broken homes.

Alcohol and drugs bring on a multitude of serious problems that impact the lives of the users and the lives of family members who love the users. Satan knows that he will have an easier job to influence the children from broken homes to accept the lure of alcohol and drugs. He also knows that the odds are in his favor that he will take many of the addicts to jail, to prison, or to their grave and that he will take the majority of his addicts to Hell with him. Christian parents, your divorce will sow the seeds for satan to reap the harvest of claiming your children.

Teenage girls from broken homes try to find comfort in pre-marital sexual relationships in the sea of sin. Children are born out of wedlock. Some of the young mothers marry the biological fathers. These marriages have a tendency to fail because they are not grounded upon Godly principles. When children are born out of wedlock, long-term heartaches and hardships await the mother and the child.

Mom and dad, do you know that your divorce will impact your grandchildren who are not yet born? You have grandchildren that are in the loins of your children. The writer of Hebrews spoke of Levi being in the loins of his father (Hebrews 7:9-10). If the consequences of your divorce results in your children walking away from God, Jesus, and the church – then the possibility exists for your children to bear your grandchildren and not rear them in the Lord. The harvest of your divorce is never ending. The harvest may even follow you, your children, and your grandchildren into eternity.

No person is exempt from the consequences of divorce. Please do not deceive yourself and think that you and your children will be exempt from the harvest of divorce.

Christian parents, satan will use your divorce in the minds of your children whereby they will question all that you have taught them about love, about living for God and our Lord Jesus, about the Word of God and the church, about being part of a loving church family. Satan will capitalize upon those questions and lead your children away from the Lord. Satan has done this over and over with children who were reared in a Christian home that fell and broke apart in divorce.

Parents, if you divorce, <u>and you remarry someone with children</u>, you open a box of real live problems that will confront you for the remainder of your life.

Then, if you and your new spouse have children, you will increase the probability of greater conflicts among the three sets of children. We will discuss some of the perpetual issues that you will step into with re-marriage and with two or three sets of children.

"You are not my momma, you cannot tell me what I can and cannot do." "You are not my daddy, you can't tell me what to do." You can expect those responses from the children of your new spouse after your honeymoon when all family members come together in the same house. The children will resent the new man or woman in the house. The extent of their rebellious actions spurred by resentment will depend upon their ages.

Teenagers will react more dramatically and aggressively. They may challenge the new parent so strong verbally that the new parent will be tempted to lose self-control and strike back physically. If a physical altercation occurs and the child is injured, a possible crime is committed. The courtrooms of America hear these kinds of cases daily.

So many teenage girls in second marriage homes turn to their boyfriends for comfort and encounter pregnancy. A whole new set of problems then confront the parents. Satan has his day with these circumstances.

You may think that your problems with the two or three sets of children will go away when the children grow up and leave home. Wrong! Your problems will just shift into a different gear.

As parents you will always want to help your family (children and step-children). There will be times when one or more of your family members will have financial needs caused from health issues, accidents, grand babies being born, loss of jobs, and the list of life's challenges goes on and on. You will help your family with their needs if you possibly can. That is what parents do.

Yes, that is what parents do, they help their children. However, children from the other marriage may not take the same view of you helping their step-siblings. They seem to have a way of remembering what you do financially for your children from your first marriage, your step-children, and your children from the second marriage. They may not express their jealousy as such, but they may very well tell you that you do more for *"your children"* or *"your step-children"* than you do for them.

The sets of children as adults may over the years quit visiting you when their step brothers and sisters are home. This mind set can escalate to the point that your children quit visiting you completely. This is sad. These thorns will pierce your heart whenever you think about your children choosing to not visit you.

Please remember what we have already discussed about when your adult child comes to you and announces they are considering divorce. There is nothing that you can say scripturally that will influence them to not divorce. However, you can share the heartaches from your divorce with them and maybe that will touch them. Allow all of the heartaches and pains from your divorce to spill out of your heart to your child. They may be influenced to reconsider their decision to divorce, commit to reconciling with their spouse, and keep their family together.

I told a brother in Christ that I was writing this book and he said to be sure and mention the hollow that divorce leaves deep in the heart of the children. He is in his late forties or early fifties and a victim of his parent's divorce. Webster defines *hollow* as a cavity, hole, depression, valley, or empty. You now as an adult would have to been a victim of divorce when you were a child to relate to the hollowness of this dear brother's heart – a hole in his heart that is empty and cannot be filled. He shared about the permanent hole within his heart that will accompany him to his grave.

Folks, I have only skimmed the surface of the waters of the harvest from divorce. The harvest from the innumerable seeds of divorce is of such magnitude and so personal to each family that it would require a library of books to be written to adequately cover the subject. I do not know why God has trusted me over the years to counsel with people who were having marital issues. Maybe it is because He knows that I love people and I have personally experienced the heartaches and aftermath of divorce. I relate to the consequences of divorce.

THERE IS NO ESCAPE FROM THE CONSEQUENCES OF DIVORCE. THE SEEDS OF DIVORCE WILL SPROUT FORTH BROKEN HEARTS, BROKEN LIVES, AND BROKEN SOULS. THE SPIRITUAL THORNS WILL REMAIN FOR GENERATIONS.

CHAPTER 8

REMARRIAGE

Jesus spoke His Father's perspective in all of His teachings. Jesus told His disciples, **"For I did not speak on My own initiative, but the Father Himself who sent Me has given Me a commandment as to what to say and what to speak"** (John 12:49). All the words that came from the mouth of Jesus during His ministry and after His resurrection were words from His Father.

What is God's perspective on men and women remarrying? God taught through Jesus His will regarding man's remarriage. We will review Jesus Christ's teachings on remarriage and learn the requirements for a second marriage to be approved by Him and His Father. A second marriage that is not approved by Jesus and His Father is a union bound in the clutches of adultery.

Jesus spoke about remarriage in His sermon on the mount, **"It hath been said, 'Whosoever shall put away his wife, let him give her a writing of divorcement: but I say unto you, That whosoever shall put away** [divorce] **his wife, saving for the cause of fornication, causeth her to commit adultery: and whosoever shall marry her that is divorced committeth adultery"** (Matthew 5:31-32, emphasis added, KJV). Jesus taught very simply and firmly that a man should not divorce his wife except if she commits fornication with another man.

Later in Jesus Christ's ministry, some Pharisees came to Jesus to test Him and they asked, "...Is it lawful for a man to divorce his wife for any reason at all?

And He answered and said, "Have you not read that He who created them from the beginning MADE THEM MALE AND FEMALE, and said, 'FOR THIS REASON A MAN SHALL LEAVE HIS FATHER AND MOTHER AND BE JOINED TO HIS WIFE, AND THE TWO SHALL BECOME ONE FLESH'?

So they are no longer two, but one flesh. What therefore God has joined together, let no man separate." They said to Him, "Why then did Moses command to GIVE HER A CERTIFICATE OF DIVORCE AND SEND *her* AWAY?"

He said to them, "Because of your hardness of heart Moses permitted you to divorce your wives; but from the beginning it has not been this way. And I say to you, whoever divorces his wife, except for immorality [fornication, KJV], and marries another woman commits adultery" (Matthew 19:3-9, emphasis added).

Jesus taught that if man divorces his wife for any reason other than fornication and the man remarries, the man commits adultery. Mark records Jesus saying the same regarding a wife, "and if she herself divorces her husband and marries another man, she is committing adultery" (Mark 10:12).

Luke recorded Jesus speaking to the Pharisees, "Everyone who divorces his wife and marries another commits adultery, and he who marries one who is divorced from a husband commits adultery" (Luke 16:18).

43

GOD HATES ADULTERY!!! God had a lot to say about marriage, adultery, homosexuality, and other ungodly relationships when God gave His law to Moses. He placed a severe penalty upon those who committed adultery. Listen to God as He spoke to Moses, **"If there is a man who commits adultery with another man's wife, one who commits adultery with his friend's wife, the adulterer and the adulteress shall surely be put to death"** (Leviticus 20:10). God's disdain for adultery was so great that He had the adulterer and the adulteress put to physical death.

> If God's penalty for adultery was a death sentence today, America would be a barren land with few inhabitants!

God still hates adultery. He still has a death sentence for the adulterer and the adulteress. The death sentence is eternal death in the fires of Hell. The apostle Paul wrote concerning God's appointed judgment upon those living in adultery today, **"Now the works of the flesh are manifest, which are these, <u>adultery, fornication</u>, uncleanness** [impurity], **lasciviousness** [sensuality], **idolatry, witchcraft** [sorcery], **hatred, variance** [strife], **emulations** [jealousy], **wrath** [outbursts of anger], **strife** [disputes], **seditions** [dissensions], **heresies, envying, murders, drunkenness, revellings** [carousing], **and such like:**

Of the which I tell you before, as I have also told you in time past, <u>that they which do such things shall not inherit the kingdom of God</u>" (Galatians 5:19-21, KJV, emphasis added).

We will now reflect upon a marriage whereby one spouse is a Christian and the other spouse is an unbeliever. Paul instructed the brethren in Corinth regarding such a marriage of a believer and an unbeliever. **"But to the married I give instructions, not I, but the Lord, that the wife should not leave her husband (but if she does leave, she must remain unmarried, or else be reconciled to her husband), and that the husband should not divorce his wife.**

But to the rest I say, not the Lord, that if any brother has a wife who is an unbeliever, and she consents to live with him, he must not divorce her.

And a woman who has an unbelieving husband and he consents to live with her, she must not send her husband away.

For the unbelieving husband is sanctified through his wife, and the unbelieving wife is sanctified through her believing husband; for otherwise your children are unclean, but now they are holy.

Yet if the unbelieving one leaves, let him leave, the brother or the sister is not under bondage in such cases, but God has called us to peace" (1 Corinthians 7:10-15). *"The brother or the sister is not under bondage in such cases"* in verse 15 must be kept in context with verse 10. Paul is saying that the Christian spouse is not under bondage to remain married to the nonbeliever. He is not giving the brother or sister the right to remarry. People take this verse out of context to justify themselves in remarriage.

God still hates adultery. He still has a death sentence for the adulterer and the adulteress. The death sentence is eternal death in the fires of Hell.

Allow us now to consider the Christian widow or widower. Are they permitted by Scripture to remarry? Yes, they are. Paul wrote, **"A wife is bound as long as her husband lives; but if her husband is dead, she is free to be married to whom she wishes, <u>only in the Lord</u>"** (1 Corinthians 7:39, underline added for emphasis). **"For the married woman is bound by law to her husband while he is living; but if her husband dies, she is released from the law concerning the husband.**

So then, if while her husband is living she is joined to another man, she shall be called an adulteress; but if her husband dies, she is free from the law, so that she is not an adulteress though she is joined to another man" (Romans 7:2-3). Paul through the inspiration of the Holy Spirit instructed that a Christian widow can remarry, BUT only in the Lord. She must marry a Christian man who does not have adultery hanging over his head from a previous scripturally unjustified divorce. The same would be true for a widower.

What about the Christian man or woman who has gone through a scripturally justified divorce and desires to remarry? They should remarry a Christian. Please listen to Paul, **"Do not be bound together with unbelievers; for what partnership have righteousness and lawlessness, or what fellowship has light with darkness"** (2 Corinthians 6:14). *Bad company corrupts good morals.* Paul said for Christians to not bind themselves together with an unbeliever in any close relationship. The relationship may be a bosom friend, or in a business venture together, or in marriage, or may be a recreational (fishing/hunting) partner. A Christian is not to enter into a marriage union and bind himself/herself together with an unbeliever.

To those of you who experienced divorce and you had scriptural justification for your divorce, I offer the following words of encouragement. Beg God to help you suppress the desires of your flesh and to select a Christian spouse that has a personal relationship with God and His Son, Jesus Christ – to select someone who has a kindred spirit with your spirit. Please look at their inward beauty, not the beauty of their body.

Seek and find someone with a servant's heart who will serve the Lord along beside you, whereby the two of you are one in Christ and are His workmanship created in Christ Jesus for good works. Select someone who will glorify God with their life and who will encourage you and lift you up in the Lord constantly. That special person is out there somewhere waiting on you. Please petition God to introduce you to that special person. Then wait on God and allow Him time to unite the two of you. Remember that God is not on a time schedule like you and me.

There have been and are many married couples who have been converted to Christ in their second marriage and they each had no scriptural justification for their divorce from their first spouse. They find themselves in a soul-threatening dilemma. This remarriage issue has challenged church leaders for decades in their spiritual shepherding of these

Christians. We shall leave man's opinion out of this discussion and focus upon Scriptural facts in the context of this remarriage issue.

Precious brother and sister in Christ, if you are living in a second marriage with these circumstances, please understand that the following words are spoken with extreme, genuine love for you and your soul. I beg you to open your mind and your heart to fully receive, understand, and accept God's Word on this subject.

Let us consider the following Scriptural facts:
- ➢ If there is no Scriptural justification for the divorce in the first marriage, then the man and woman are living in adultery in their second marriage (Matt. 19:3-9).

- ➢ Jesus did not approve of or condone an adulterous marriage nor did He teach that such a marriage can become right in the eyes of God under any circumstances.

- ➢ A Christian may repent of their adultery and in faith ask God for forgiveness of adultery and be forgiven for that sin. Forgiveness will not be enjoyed without repentance. When the Christian continues to live in an adulterous marriage, they repeat the sin of adultery over and over.

➢ Paul addressed the issue of continuing to live in sin, **"What shall we say then? Are we to continue in sin so that grace may increase? May it never be! How shall we who died to sin still live in it?"** (Romans 6:1-2).

➢ There is no Scripture that states that the forgiveness of the sin of adultery makes a marriage right before God. A marriage that is an adulterous union will remain that way. God made no allowance for an adulterous marriage to become approved in His sight when both husband and wife are converted to Christ. His approval of such is just not found in the Scriptures. Man is the one who makes the approval. You know and I know that man does not have the authority to add to or take away from God's Word or to make any change in His Word.

➢ Sweet brother and sister in Christ, the following Scriptures may jolt you. They are presented to you with love for your souls. The writer of the book of Hebrews taught, **"For if we go on sinning willfully after receiving the knowledge of the truth, there no longer remains a sacrifice for sins, But a terrifying expectation of judgment and THE FURY OF A FIRE WHICH WILL CONSUME THE ADVERSARIES"** (Hebrews 10:26-27).

We come to a fork in the road of life when we are made aware of sin in our life and we learn from the Word that our sin is condemned in the eyes of God – this fork in the road demands a choice. We either choose to remain in sin or we choose to repent, beg God's forgiveness, and turn from sin. When we choose to willfully remain in sin, the blood that our Lord Jesus shed for our sins and His death becomes in vain for us, because His self-sacrifice no longer atones for our sins.

Do you see that continuing in an adulterous marriage is remaining in sin willfully? Please listen to more words of teaching in Hebrews, **"For in the case of those who have once been enlightened and have tasted of the heavenly gift and have been made partakers of the Holy Spirit, And have tasted the good word of God and the powers of the age to come, and then have fallen away, it is impossible to renew them again to repentance, since they again crucify to themselves the Son of God and put Him to open shame"** (Hebrews 6:4-6).

Sweet brethren, if you are living in an adulterous marriage, please pray to our Father God for Him to help you make the right decision regarding your marriage. If you choose to remove yourselves from your adulterous marriage, God and His Son will comfort you in the painful process of making things right before Him. Jesus will give you the strength to bear the heartbreaking pain of removing yourselves from your adulterous marriage (Philippians 4:13).

We all have to live with the consequences of our choices. Some of the consequences are so heartbreaking that we have great difficulty facing what we must do to make things right with God. May God have mercy upon all of us who call ourselves Christians! We are sinners in need of the cleansing blood of the Lamb, Jesus Christ. The more we learn of His will, the more we realize how much we are in need of God's grace and mercy. May God have mercy upon us!

Dear brother and sister, please study God's Word diligently together and beg God for wisdom and understanding. Remain in prayer and come to a reconciliation of what you must do to be pleasing to God in your personal marriage circumstances. May your actions and your resolve be based upon the foundation of God's Word. You will be thankful that you took that approach when you enter the gates of Heaven.

PLEASE KEEP READING.

What about the Christian man or woman who has gone through a scripturally justified divorce and desires to remarry? They should remarry a Christian. Please listen to Paul, **"Do not be bound together with unbelievers; for what partnership have righteousness and lawlessness, or what fellowship has light with darkness"** (2 Corinthians 6:14). *Bad company corrupts good morals.* Paul said for Christians to not bind themselves together with an unbeliever in any close relationship. The relationship/partnership may be a bosom friend or be in a business venture together or in marriage or a recreational partner. A Christian is not to enter into a marriage union and bind himself/herself together with an unbeliever.

CHAPTER 9

FORGIVE, RECONCILE, and RESTORE

Have you ever found yourself in a real life-threatening storm and you were faced with only two ways of escape? Then you are warned that one road leads to disaster and that the other road will be rough, stressful traveling but you can survive and escape the storm.

My great-grandson, Landon, and I planned a fishing trip last summer to Bolivar peninsula across the bay from Galveston, Texas. It took days for me to get caught up on my work so that I could take a week off and fish. During that time I failed to watch any weather reports which proved to be a big, big mistake. The day came for our departure and we left for the Gulf of Mexico with enough gear to open a fishing tackle shop. Our visions of catching trophy trout and flounder magnified as we traveled toward Bolivar.

We bypassed Houston to the east and traveled to the east end of the peninsula. Suddenly we left the mainland and we were on the peninsula with the waters of the Gulf of Mexico close to the road. What an experience for two highlanders to see water to the horizon and to hear the roar of God's waves as they washed upon the beach!

Then something happened. My truck motor lost its power. The motor did not quit, it just went into an idle mode. We were creeping along. I pulled over on the shoulder of the road and killed the engine. "What do I do now?" Our joy flew away with the Gulf wind. I started the engine, it sounded normal and I could accelerate. We resumed our journey, but not for long. The engine began to perform for a few feet, a few yards, or maybe a mile or so. It took forever to travel to our destination, one of my friend's tourist houses on the west end of the peninsula.

The next morning we were up early and eager to fish. The resident property manager of my friend's rental units said that he would be glad to guide us and put us on fish. We accepted his offer. Off we went to buy live bait and then to the guide's fishing spot on the inter-coastal waters. Landon caught his first trout and it was bragging size. We were really enjoying our sea water fishing adventure.

Then something happened. Storm clouds began to gather. The wind increased to the point that it was difficult to stand without bracing yourself. Then lightning began. Our guide said that we needed to get off the water immediately because of the lightning. So we loaded our stuff in the truck and left to go eat lunch at a local café. We hoped that the storm would pass and we could resume fishing later in the day.

The guide's cell phone began to ring while we ate lunch. The County emergency broadcast was sent to all the residents of the peninsula advising everyone to evacuate the peninsula immediately because of the approaching tropical storm from the Gulf. Bolivar was on the eastern side of the counter clockwise rotation of the storm winds. Waters would be pushed from the Gulf upon the land of the peninsula.

We finished our lunch and went back to our guest house. The guide continued to receive phone calls from the County with updates on the approaching storm. Family members from the mainland were calling him, encouraging him to leave Bolivar. His wife came home from work. They showed more concern for us than they did for themselves and they helped us move our belongings from the house to the truck.

There are only two exits off the peninsula. You can go east on the road to the mainland (which is the route that we entered the peninsula) or you can cross over the Galveston Bay on a ferry boat to Galveston. The last County emergency broadcast said that the Gulf waters were already over the road to the east just before you reach the mainland. People were being warned not to attempt that exit to the east, but to go west on the ferry to Galveston. The broadcast warned that it was unknown how much longer the ferries would be in operation because the ferries would have to shut down when the waters of the bay became too rough. We chose to take the ferry to Galveston.

People of Bolivar had responded in a positive manner to the storm warnings and were trying to leave the peninsula. It was a long wait to get on a ferry. The fury of the storm was increasing. I was praying that we would be able to cross the bay before the ferries had to moor down and ride out the storm. God allowed us to board a ferry. The waters of the bay were already extremely rough. The rain became so hard and torrential as we crossed the bay that we could not see the waters of the bay in front of the ferry. God delivered us safely to the shore of Galveston.

It seemed that all of the people in Galveston were fleeing from the storm. Traffic was bumper-to-bumper leaving Galveston. My old truck started its routine of losing power again and I had to work my way into the right lane. The next hour was one of the most stressful times this old fellow has ever experienced on earth. The traffic was at its maximum, a reflection of the people fleeing from danger, and my old truck kept losing its power. I would have to pull over on the shoulder of the road, kill the motor, wait, and then start again. And then wait and wait for an opening in the right lane so that I could pull back on the road and go a short distance more.

We finally made it to the freeway that bypasses Houston to the east and goes to Texas City. We headed toward Texas City and the old truck began to go shorter distances each time before the motor lost power. I asked Landon to find my cell phone and call two precious brothers in Christ in Winnsboro, Texas, and tell them about the truck; that we were in trying to flee the storm; and ask them to pray for us so that God would keep our old truck motor running and we could safely escape the path of the storm. We were successful at contacting both of the men.

My great-grandson and I saw God's answer to our brethren's prayers (we learned later that they also asked more brethren to pray for us). The old truck would only travel a few yards at a time. I was trying to keep from being run over by the crazy traffic. The shoulder of the road became our safe haven. Shortly after God's children started praying for us, I cranked the engine, found a break in the traffic and pulled upon the road. The engine sounded normal again. I put my foot into the accelerator and here we went. The engine ran as if new for the next few hours and delivered us out of the path of the storm. Praise God! Praise God! There is power in prayer.

You may be asking "Why, why did he start the last chapter with this story?" That is a good question. Do you remember the question that I opened this chapter with? *Have you ever found yourself in a real life-threatening storm and you were faced with only two ways of escape? Then you are warned that one road leads to disaster and that the other road will be rough, stressful traveling but you can survive and escape the storm.*

Precious brother and sister in Christ, the life-threatening storm represents your marital problems and issues that you are in the midst of. There are only two roads leading away from the troubled waters of your marriage problems - the road of reconciliation or the road of divorce. You have been warned that divorce is disaster. The consequences of divorce will follow you through your life on earth and maybe even into eternity because satan will use the divorce to try to claim your soul and the souls of your children and grandchildren.

Reconciliation is the route to survival and recovery. God is a God of reconciliation. He reconciled mankind to Himself through the blood of His Son Jesus. God gave His Son so that we may be reconciled to Him, God our Father. He wants you to be reconciled with your spouse. You can take the Highway of Holiness and allow God to help you work through your relationship issues.

" A highway will be there,
A roadway, and it will be called
The Highway of Holiness.
The unclean will not Travel on it,
But it will be for him
Who walks that way,
And fools will not
Wander on it"
(Isaiah 35:8).

God loves you and your children and He honors your marriage. Turn your relationship over to God and allow Him to heal you. He will help you to reconcile and restore your relationship. But first, you must forgive one another and then ask God for His forgiveness (Matthew 6:14-15). Permit God's Word, love, and grace to clear the clouds of your marital relationship. God will deliver you from the storm with your marriage intact, whole, and well.

Mom and dad, if you are believers in Christ as the Son of God; you believe that God raised Jesus from the dead; and you have been baptized into Christ for the remission of your sins; then you have been blessed with the gift of the Holy Spirit – the indwelling of the Holy Spirit (Acts 2:38). **"Or do you not know that your body is a temple of the Holy Spirit who is in you, whom you have from God, and that you are not your own?**

For you have been bought with a price: therefore glorify God in your body" (1 Corinthians 6:19-20).

"Do you not know that you are a temple of God and that the Spirit of God dwells in you? If any man destroys the temple of God, God will destroy him, for the temple of God is holy, and that is what you are" (1 Corinthians 3:16-17).

Christian mom and dad, you are special people in the eyes of God. You belong to Him. Your body, mind, and soul belong to God. Your body is the temple of God and the temple of His Holy Spirit. Your body is not yours to do with as you please. Your body is not yours to have sex with anyone but your spouse. Your marriage union is just as precious to God as your body is to Him for your marriage is ordained by Him.

We are to walk by the Spirit. Please listen to the apostle Paul, **"But I say, walk by the Spirit, and you will not carry out the desire of the flesh"** (Galatians 5:16). Our daily walk in our marriage relationship is to be a walk by the Spirit. We will not submit to the desires of the flesh when we walk with the Holy Spirit and when we allow Him to perform His ministry in our lives. Marital issues arise when we turn our eyes away from the Lord and we fail to walk by the Spirit.

We are to allow the Spirit to lead us through the medium of God's Word for the Word is the sword of the Spirit (Ephesians 6:17). **"For all who are being led by the Spirit of God, these are sons of God"** (Romans 8:14). We must study God's Word so that we may know His will for our lives and so we may know the commandments of Christ. We are blessed by our Father God with the avenue of prayer. We can pray for wisdom and understanding of His Word. He will grant us understanding.

We must not mistreat the Holy Spirit by grieving Him. Israel grieved the Holy Spirit as recorded by Isaiah, **"But they rebelled and grieved His Holy Spirit; therefore He turned Himself to become their enemy, He fought against them"** (Isaiah 63:10).

God takes a very dim view of His children grieving the Holy Spirit. Actually, this is an understatement because He reacted toward Israel's grieving the Holy Spirit by turning from being their protector to becoming their enemy. God had exercised extreme forbearance with the Israelites in their reckless spiritual living. He had been compassionate, had forgiven them, had restrained His anger and not destroyed them. They grieved Him in the desert but He did not react towards them in this offense like He did when they grieved the Holy Spirit.

"Do not grieve the Holy Spirit of God, by whom you were sealed for the day of redemption" (Ephesians 4:30). The Holy Spirit is grieved when our actions are not in harmony with God's will; when we walk contrary to His commandments; when we live for the flesh and walk in the darkness. There is no middle ground. We either walk in the Light or we walk in the darkness for there is no spiritual twilight. We either walk in the Spirit or we walk in the flesh.

Divorce grieves the Holy Spirit. We have established by Scripture that God hates divorce. Therefore Christian married couples grieve God when they divorce. When Christians grieve God with their actions, the Holy Spirit who indwells within them is grieved. Please, please do not divorce and grieve God and the Holy Spirit.

FORGIVE   So many marriages fail because one spouse succumbs to the desire of the flesh and has sexual relations with someone outside of their marriage. The spouse that commits adultery sets their mind on the flesh. Paul said this is death, spiritual death. **"For the mind set on the flesh is death, but the mind set on the Spirit is life and peace"** (Romans 8:6). God will forgive the spouse that commits adultery whenever they truly repent and seek His forgiveness.

Jesus instructed us to forgive others for their transgressions so that our heavenly Father will forgive us and if we do not forgive others, our Father will not forgive us of our transgressions (Matthew 6:14-15).

Please forgive your spouse fully in your heart and seek to reconcile. This is what Jesus wants you to do. Forgive your spouse.

Let us share some Scripture to together to reflect further upon forgiving, reconciling, and restoring. The apostle Paul taught, **"Therefore be imitators of God, as beloved children; and walk in love, just as Christ also loved you and gave Himself up for us, an offering and a sacrifice to God as a fragrant aroma"** (Ephesians 5:1-2).

What a challenge Paul gave us - to be an imitator of God! We have the ability to imitate our Father God, or Paul would not have instructed us to. Please remember, Paul was filled with the Holy Spirit when he wrote to the Church at Ephesus. The Holy Spirit is the Spirit of Truth (John 15:26, John 16:13), therefore, Paul spoke with truth with his instruction for us to imitate God.

Paul wrote to the church of the Thessalonians in God the Father and the Lord Jesus Christ (1 Thessalonians 1:1) and confirmed that the brethren had become imitators of the Lord, **"You also became imitators of us and of the Lord, having received the word in much tribulation with the joy of the Holy Spirit"** (1 Thessalonians 1:6). Those Christians achieved being imitators of God. We can do the same.

WE MUST KNOW GOD TO IMITATE GOD

To be an imitator of God,
We have to know God.
To know God, we must first desire to know Him.
We have to study His Word,
To learn His heart, His nature,
To learn His will for
Our obedience unto Him.

To know God,
Our heart, mind, and soul must be filled
With love for God and for our fellowman.
Knowing God is more than
Just knowing about Him.

To know God,
We can observe His creation,
Learn of Him and His awesome power and
His perfection in all that He created.
Learn of His attention to detail in His creation,
Learn that He did not create at random
But all of His creation has a purpose.

God's mountains, oceans, beaches, valleys, clouds
Are all testimony to His love for beautiful surroundings.
He watches over His creation constantly,
He enjoys the beauty of His creation.

FORGIVE, RECONCILE, and RESTORE

God's power to create
Is seen in mothers giving birth to their children,
Is seen in animals giving birth to their young,
Is seen in the farmer's seed sprouting forth
To provide man with food.

We know God
Through all that He does spiritually
In our lives daily.
He gave us Jesus,
Who shed His precious blood
So we may have soul salvation.

Jesus Christ gave us His church,
So we may have a family of like-kind believers,
So we may not walk alone
In our journey through this land.

God gave us His Word, the Scriptures, to learn His way.
He sent the Holy Spirit to convict us of our sins.
He gave us the gift of the Holy Spirit upon
Our baptism into Christ for the remission of our sins.
The Holy Spirit has His assigned ministry from God
To be our Comforter and our Helper.

We know God
Through all that He does in our
Physical lives constantly.
He promised that the righteous will not go hungry,
He keeps His promise daily.
Through His Spirit, He gives us
The ability to work and provide for our family.

He sustains our physical needs daily.
He protects us underneath the shelter of His wings.
We believe that He is
The one and only true living God.

He is our loving Father
Who surrounds us with His blessings
Every moment, every breath of our life.
He desires that we know Him,
He desires our love, our devotion,
Our drawing near to Him,
Our communication with Him,
Our dependence upon Him constantly,
Our taking refuge in Him.

May we each desire to know Him more fully,
Desire to love Him above ourselves,
To love Him to the very maximum of our ability,
Desire to serve Him more diligently,
To walk with Him regardless of the cost,
Desire to be His child and His bond-servant,
Desire to tell the story of Jesus
To everyone who will listen.

Precious child of God,
Please take time to learn of God,
To know Him Through His Word,
Through His Creation,
Through your experiences with Him.
Rise beyond knowing about Him, Know Him!
Become an Imitator of God.

Jim Hampton

To imitate God, we must know God. ***Do you know about God? Or do you know God?*** There is a difference, a huge difference with a possible eternal consequence for not knowing God. Knowing God is more than professing to know God. The apostle Paul addressed those who profess to know God, **"To the pure, all things are pure; but to those who are defiled and unbelieving, nothing is pure, but both their mind and their conscience are defiled. <u>They profess to know God, but by their deeds they deny Him,</u> being detestable and disobedient and worthless for any good deed"** (Titus 1:15-16, underline added for emphasis). Our deeds are testimony to whether we truly know God or our claim to know Him is just merely lip service.

We learn through the Scriptures that God is:
- A God of Love - 1 John 4:7-8.
- A God of Holiness - 1 Peter 1:14-16.
- A God filled with Loving Kindness - Psalm 36:10; Psalm 103:11, 17; Psalm 145:17
- A Forgiving God - Matthew 6:14-15.
- A Merciful God - 2 Corinthians 1:3.
- A God of Light - 1 John 1:5.
- A God of Peace - 1 Thessalonians 5:23.
- A God of Compassion - Psalm 25:6.
- A God of Humility - Proverbs 22:4.
- A God of Gentleness - Philippians 4:4-5.
- A God who has a special place in His heart for Orphans and Widows - Psalm 68:5.
- A God of Hope - Romans 15:13.
- A God of Wisdom - James 1:5.
- A God of Knowledge - 1 Samuel 2:3.

> A God of Understanding - Psalm 119:27, 34, 125, 169.
> A God who is Immutable - James 1:17, Malachi 3:6
> A God of all Grace - 1 Peter 5:10.
> A God of all Comfort - 2 Corinthians 1:3.
> A God of Wrath - Colossians 3:6.
> A God of Justice - Psalm 89:14.
> A God of Forbearance - Romans 2:4; 3:25 (KJV).
> A God of Longsuffering - 2 Peter 3:9 (KJV).
> A God of Righteousness - Psalm 11:7; Psalm 97:6; Psalm 145:17.
> A God of Purity - Psalm 12:6; Psalm 19:8.
> A God of Truth - Psalm 25:4, 10; Psalm 40:11.
> A God of Faithfulness - Psalm 33:4.
> God is Gracious - Psalm 111:4; Psalm 86:15; Psalm 116:5.
> God is a Rock - Deut. 32:3-4, 18; Psalm 18:2.
> God is a Fortress - Psalm 18:2; Psalm 144:2.
> God is a Deliverer - Psalm 18:2; Psalm 144:2.
> God is a Refuge - Psalm 144:2.
> God is a Shield - Psalm 18:2, Psalm 144:2.
> God is a Horn of Salvation - Psalm 18:2.
> God is a Stronghold - Psalm 18:2; Psalm 144:2.

We shall first consider God's attribute of love that we must imitate. John through the inspiration of the Holy Spirit wrote that if we do not love, we do not know God for God is love.

"Beloved, let us love one another, for love is from God; and everyone who loves is born of God and knows God. The one who does not love does not know God, for God is love" (1 John 4:7-8).

We must first love God with all of our heart, mind, and soul and love our neighbor as we love our self, before we can know God. A lawyer came to Jesus and asked Him a question, **"Teacher, which is the great commandment in the Law? And He** [Jesus] **said to him, 'YOU SHALL LOVE THE LORD YOUR GOD WITH ALL YOUR HEART, AND WITH ALL YOUR SOUL, AND WITH ALL YOUR MIND.'**
This is the great and foremost commandment. The second is like it, 'YOU SHALL LOVE YOUR NEIGHBOR AS YOURSELF' " (Matthew 22:36-39, emphasis added).

Our heart, mind, and soul must be filled with love for one another, for all mankind, even our enemies. Jesus instructed us to love our enemies and pray for those who persecute us (Matthew 5:44).

Love is the very foundation upon which we build our knowledge of God. We do not know God if we have not love for our fellow man, therefore, we cannot be imitators of God. Our Father God is the supreme example of Love for us to imitate. **"For God so loved the world, that He gave His only begotten Son, that whoever believes in Him shall not perish, but have eternal life"** (John 3:16).

John gave additional insight into God's love for us, **"By this the love of God was manifested in us, that God has sent His only begotten Son into the world so that we might live through Him.**

In this is love, not that we loved God, but that He loved us and sent His Son *to be* **the propitiation [atonement] for our sins. Beloved, if God so loved us, we also ought to love one another."** (1 John 4:9-11, emphasis added). Who among our Christian family today would freely give their only son to suffer harsh physical abuse, be nailed to a cross, and die a painful death for people who loved not the son or the parent? Our human minds cannot fully comprehend the depth of God's love that motivated Him to give His only Son for man's soul salvation and eternal life. However, we can plead to God to give us a greater understanding of His love and ask Him to help us develop an endless love in our hearts for our fellow man.

Christian husband, love your wife as yourself. Christian wife, love your husband as yourself. Please forgive one another for whatever actions and behaviors that have caused your marriage issues. IMITATE GOD, LOVE AND FORGIVE ONE ANOTHER. Love your children as yourselves and keep your home together for them and for you. Other than your souls, your children are your most precious assets. Please do not destroy their lives by divorce.

Precious brother and sister in Christ, I beg you to not be persuaded by the world's view of divorce. The world views the marriage union as no more than a disposable relationship. Christians are not to think as the world thinks and are not to conform to this world, but be transformed by the renewing of their minds. *"Therefore I urge you, brethren, by the mercies of God, to present your bodies a living and holy sacrifice, acceptable to God, which is your spiritual service of worship. And do not be conformed to this world, but be transformed by the renewing of your mind, so that you may prove what the will of God is, that which is good and acceptable and perfect"* (Romans 12:1-2).

I want to share with you a message from a book by Spiros Zodhiates, Th.D, titled, "May I Divorce & Remarry? He taught about being legally right but morally wrong by following the ways of the world in divorce. He built his lesson on this subject upon 1 Corinthians 7:11, *"But if she does leave, she must remain unmarried, or else be reconciled to her husband: and that the husband should not divorce his wife."*

Speaking about the Corinthian community, he wrote, "It was so easy, however, for the Christian community to be affected by civil or state law, even as it is today. Christians may think that because the civil law permits divorce that that is adequate justification to proceed to divorce one's spouse. One may be led astray by something that may be legally right to do, but morally wrong. Through civil law, society has often established moral standards which do not agree with scriptural standards. In Corinth, Paul was establishing the scriptural standards by which marriage should be regulated. Since we live in a similar multi-ethnic and multi-cultural society and the judicial system is totally non-religious, it is so easy for us to be affected by the laws of the land and to try to justify what the law permits as morally correct just because it is permitted by the courts" (Pages 115-116).

Precious Christian husband and Christian wife, *"There is a way which seems right to a man, but its end is the way of death".* ₁ Please do not follow the ways of society and throw away your marriage. Forgive, reconcile, and restore. Keep your family together. Weather the storm and the sunshine of life will follow. Keep your marriage based upon a solid foundation, the foundation of God, your rock and your salvation.₂

Draw near to God. Draw near to Jesus. Draw near to one another. Cast your burdens upon the Lord. **"Cast your burden upon the Lord and He will sustain you; He will never allow the righteous to be shaken"** (Psalm 55:22). In faith, lay your burdens at the feet of Jesus. Pick up your cross and follow Him. Empty yourself of self. Ask God to help you overcome yourself. Fill your heart, mind, and soul with love for God, love for Jesus, love for your spouse, and love for your children. Imitate Jesus and consider the lives and the best interest of your spouse and your children before you think of yourself, keep your family together.

Both of you take refuge in Jesus, the Son of God. **"Do homage to the Son, that He not become angry, and you perish in the way, for His wrath may soon be kindled. How blessed are all who take refuge in Him!"** (Psalm 2:12). Place yourselves and your union in the hands of

Jesus. He will heal your hearts. He will heal your union. Place your trust in Him.

> **"...But he who trusts in the Lord,**
> **Loving kindness shall surround him.**
> **Be glad in the Lord and rejoice,**
> **You righteous ones;**
> **And shout for joy,**
> **All you who are upright in heart"**
> (Psalm 32:10-11).

> **"Trust in the Lord with all your heart**
> **And do not lean on your own understanding"**
> (Proverbs 3:5).

Oh, how you need wisdom at this crossroads in your life. Please ask God for wisdom. You must ask in faith. He will generously give you wisdom when you ask in faith, believing that He will answer your prayer.[3] His wisdom from above is pure, peaceable, gentle, reasonable, full of mercy and good fruits, unwavering, and without hypocrisy.[4] Precious husband and wife, please read the first eight chapters of Proverbs together. You will learn the value of wisdom in your lives.

Satan sees his opportunity for victory when a Christian couple has marital issues. He will go to work to harden the hearts of the couple. This is a ploy of satan that has worked over-and- over for him. Examine your heart. Perform a spiritual x-ray of your heart. Be brutally honest with yourself. If you discover that your heart has hardened, please pray that God will grant you a "spiritual heart transplant." Please, please, get your heart right with God, right with Jesus, and right with your spouse. When your heart is right, healing of your marriage will begin.

> Please forgive your spouse fully in your heart and seek to reconcile. This is what Jesus wants you to do. Forgive your spouse.

You must not expect the wounds from your marital issues to heal overnight. They will heal with God's help and your marriage union will be stronger than ever. We will close this book with some practical recommendations to enhance your marriage healing process.

- ➤ Approach your marital issues head-on. Do not run from them.
- ➤ Admit to one another that you have marital problems.
- ➤ Commit to God and to one another that you will work through your problems with help from God and from Jesus and with love for one another.
- ➤ Commit to one another that you will lay your problems at the feet of Jesus.
- ➤ Resolve that you will not argue.
- ➤ Resolve that you will not raise your voices at one another.
- ➤ Resolve that you will restrain from anger and that you will retain self-control.
- ➤ Resolve that your children will not hear your marital problems.

> Resolve that your children are your second greatest asset (your soul is your greatest asset) and that you will overcome your relationship issues to keep your family together and to give your children a Christian mom and a Christian dad and a loving Christian home.

The "stage is set now" to begin your healing process. Communication with each other is critical. Begin to communicate and pray with one another and remain in that mode. You each take turns to pray aloud. Share your grievances with one another. Ask God to help you to drill through your complaints into your hearts and minds to understand the root of your problems.

The nature of the root problem or problems will determine the action to take for recovery. The first action to take is to pray with all of your heart, mind, and soul in faith. Beg God to help you overcome, to help you heal. Your second action is to take responsibility for your behavior that brought you to this point in life. Then repent and beg God's forgiveness and resolve to correct your behavior with the help of the Lord. And then waste no time in proceeding with making things right.

It is difficult for many couples to communicate with one another; to pray with one another; to come to an understanding of the root to their problems; and then to take action to make corrections and reconcile. They step around facing their issues with one another. Their lack of facing their marital issues together is fatal to many marriages. Please, please do not choose to be among this number.

I have known Christian couples who have divorced over one spouse being addicted to prescription drugs; one spouse abusing credit cards and running up debt; dangerous attitude of the husband toward the wife's children from the first marriage; one spouse committing adultery; one spouse who did not want the responsibilities of being a wife and mother; one spouse who wanted to be "free" after her children were grown and away from home. Oh, how the actions of those individuals and their divorces hurt the heart of God and the heart of our Lord Jesus and the hearts of their children. God is greater than any of these brethren's issues. God could have resolved these problems if the couples had gone to Him and laid their problems at His feet.

Christian husband and wife, the apostle Paul instructed to, **"Bear one another's burdens, and thereby fulfill the law of Christ"** (Galatians 6:2). We fulfill the law of Christ when we walk in His commandments and bear one another's burdens. Please take note of what Paul did not say. He did not say, *"Bear one another's burdens until you get tired of doing so!"* He put no time limit or restraint upon bearing one another's burdens.

"Now we who are strong ought to bear the weaknesses of those without strength and not just please ourselves" (Romans 15:1). Remember my Brethren, you can do all things that are right in the sight of God through Him who strengthens you (Philippians 4:13).

We are charged with the responsibility to bear one another's burdens. We help one another work through the personal faults that challenge the marriage. We walk together down the path of reconciliation and restoration. We walk in love for our God and for one another. We keep our family together. We are one in Christ.

TIPS FOR YOUR UNION AFTER RECONCILIATION

Begin to spend quality time together. Select a night every week to go out on a special date together. Husband, make your precious wife feel like a queen. Treat her with royalty. Dine her, court her, love her. Let her know that God and Jesus are first in your life and that she follows right behind them. Remember, she is one-half of you. The two of you make one.

Begin to pray together. Each of you pray aloud. Pray for your marriage, pray for your children, pray for your family unit.

Appoint a time each evening (except on the night of your date) to read the book of Psalms together. Take turns reading aloud. Discuss the message of the Psalms. Pray for God to bless you with an understanding of the Psalms and allow the message to sink deep within your mind and soul.

Go to the book of 1 John after you finish Psalms. After you study 1 John, please continue to read the Word together daily until God takes one of you to your eternal home.

Spend quality time with your family. Carve out time for family devotionals daily (have your family devo before you go on your date). Encourage every member of your family to pray aloud. Teach and train your children to pray from the time they can understand what you are teaching them.

Begin to have regular family outings. Create precious memories in the minds of your children – memories they will cherish long after you are gone from this earth.

Let your children know how much mom & dad love one another. Allow your love to be shown in ways other than words.

Refrain from being a "fault finder." Become an encourager.

Help one another with chores around home.

Participate together in a hobby that you both enjoy. Such activity is pleasurable and a sweet balm for the healing of your marriage. My wife and I were "crafters" before crafting became popular. When craft decor became a fad, we made craft décor items in volume and attended craft shows in central and east Texas, north Louisiana and southwest Arkansas. We had so many good times together. We now enjoy the memories of our experiences together.

Husband, tell your wife how much you love her everyday – show her by your actions. *"Husbands, love your wives, just as Christ also loved the church and gave Himself up for her...So husbands ought also to love their own wives as their own bodies.*

He who loves his own wife loves himself; for no one ever hated his own flesh, but nourishes and cherishes it, just as Christ also does the church" (Ephesians 5:25, 28-29).

Wife, tell your husband how much you love him everyday – show him by your actions. *"Older women likewise are to be reverent in their behavior...so that they may encourage the young* *__women to love their husbands__, to love their children, to be sensible, pure, workers at home, kind, being subject to their own husbands, so that the word of God will not be dishonored"* (Titus 2:3-5, underline added for emphasis).

"Above all, keep fervent in your love for one another, because love covers a multitude of sins" (1 Peter 4:8).

You have a choice. You can choose to forgive your spouse, to reconcile with your spouse, and to restore your marriage. You can choose not to pierce your spouse, yourself, and your children's souls, hearts, and minds with the spiritual thorns from the seeds of divorce.

Resolve that your children are your second greatest asset (your soul is your greatest asset) and that you will overcome your relationship issues to keep your family together and to give your children a Christian mom and a Christian dad and a loving Christian home. PLEASE, PLEASE DO NOT DIVORCE.

1 Proverbs 14:12
2 Psalm 62:2, 6-7
3 James 1:5-6
4 James 3:17

34895704R00047

Made in the USA
San Bernardino, CA
09 June 2016